EXPERIMENT WITH AIR

Written by **Bryan Murphy**

Science Consultant Dr Christine Sutton
Nuclear Physics Department, University of Oxford
Education Consultant Ruth Bessant

FRANKLIN WATTS
in association with
TWO-CAN

First published in this edition 1991 by:

Franklin Watts
96 Leonard Street
London EC2A 4RH

Copyright © Two-Can Publishing Ltd, 1991
Text copyright © Bryan Murphy, 1991
Design by Linda Blakemore.

Printed in Italy by Amadeus - Rome

The JUMP! logo and the word JUMP! are registered trade marks.

A CIP cataloguing record for this book is available from the
British Library.

ISBN: Experiment with Air 0-7496-0336-4

All photographs are copyright © Fiona Pragoff, except for the following:
Cover ZEFA Picture Library (UK) Ltd p.8 (left) NHPA (top right) Heather Angel/Biofotos (centre) NHPA p.9 (top left) Oxford Scientific Films (centre left) NHPA p.10 ZEFA
Picture Library (UK) Ltd p.13 (left) Quadrant Picture Library (right) NHPA p.14 (top) ZEFA Picture Library (UK) Ltd p.15 (bottom) NHPA p.16 Oxford Scientific Films p.17
(top) Ann Ronan Picture Library p.18 (top) Oxford Scientific Films (bottom) Science Photo Library p.21 Quadrant Picture Library p.23 (bottom centre) ZEFA Picture Library
(UK) Ltd p.24 (top) ZEFA Picture Library (UK) Ltd p.28 (bottom) ZEFA Picture Library (UK) Ltd p.29 (top) Oxford Scientific Films (bottom) NHPA

All illustrations by Sally Kindberg. Edited by Monica Byles.

With thanks to the staff and pupils of St Thomas' C.E. Primary School, London W10

CONTENTS

All words marked in **bold** can be found in the glossary

WHAT IS AIR?

Have you ever thought about **air**? You cannot see or smell it, and you can only feel it if it is moving quickly, like the **wind**. And yet air is all around us.

Here is an experiment to weigh air. Blow up two balloons and hang one from each end of a strip of wood. Hang the centre of the strip of wood from a thread tied to the back of a chair, so that you have a pair of balloon scales. With a pin, carefully make a little hole in one of the balloons near the knot to let the air out slowly.

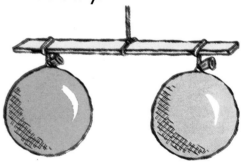

Watch what happens with your scales. Which weighs more, an empty balloon or a balloon full of air? Air weighs something. The air in a medium-sized room weighs about as much as you do.

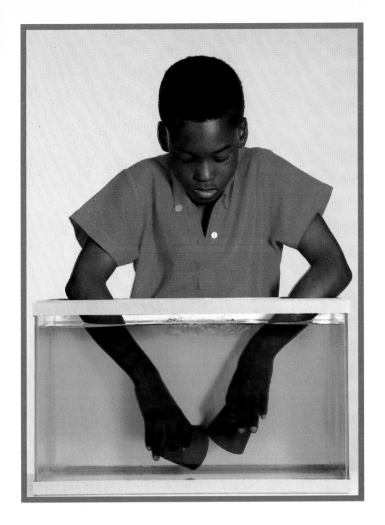

▲ You can even pour air. Fill a large plastic tank with water. Trap some air in an upside-down beaker under water and pour it upwards into another one. See if you can do this without spilling any air.

▲ When you **breathe** in, you take air into your lungs. How much air do you think your lungs hold? You can measure how much air fills your lungs by blowing through a plastic tube into a measuring jug held upside-down in a tank of water. Try it. You will be surprised how much air you breathe in and out.

◄ Candles need air to make them burn. Ask an adult to light two candles for you. Put a large jar over one, a small jar over the other. Which candle goes out first?

HEAVY AIR AND LEMONADE

There is so much air in the **atmosphere** around the Earth that it forms a heavy layer, all pushing down towards the ground. The **weight** of air pushing down on each square metre is almost the same as the weight of about 400 children. We do not feel crushed because the air all around us supports the weight of the air from above.

Tell a friend you can crush a plastic bottle without touching it. Ask an adult to pour about one cup of very hot water carefully into the bottle. Screw the lid on tightly and shake the bottle. That is all you have to do.

▼ As the air in the bottle cools down, the weight of the air outside can crush it.

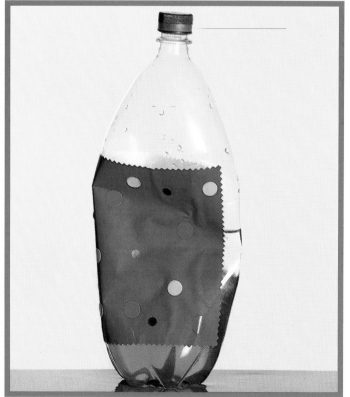

Every time you drink through a straw, you suck the air out of your mouth and make an empty space. The heavy air outside the glass then pushes on to the surface of the liquid in the bottle and pushes the drink up the straw to fill the space in your mouth.

Try sealing the straw into the mouth of the bottle with modelling clay. What happens? The heavy air cannot reach the bottle to push the liquid up the straw and you cannot drink.

7

FLYING SEEDS

When a plant makes its seeds, it needs to spread them as far as possible. There are many different sorts of seeds and just as many ways of spreading them.

▲ Some seeds have little hooks so that they can stick on to you or to passing animals. Eventually the seeds fall off and grow.

◄ Air is a very important way of scattering seeds. Some seeds are very small and can be carried far away by the wind. Can you see how?

▼ The sycamore tree has seeds at the centre of a **propeller**. When the sycamore seeds fall from the high branches, they spin slowly to the ground and can be blown far away by the wind. Do you have a sycamore tree in your area?

▼ Make your own sycamore **helicopter**. Cut out this shape from paper, fold in the bottom two flaps and weight this end with a paper clip. Throw it in the air and see what happens.

PARACHUTES

◀ When a **sky-diver** jumps out of a plane, he needs a parachute to slow him down so that he can land safely. The air drags inside the silky lining of the **parachute** and prevents gravity from tugging it so fast to the ground.

Never try to jump from a great height yourself: it is very dangerous.

▶ Sometimes, large crates of supplies are dropped out of aeroplanes in rocky or hilly places where it is too difficult to land. The parachute has to be big to slow the heavy load down as it falls. But if the parachute is too big, the supplies may drift in the air and not land in the right place.

◀ Returning from the Moon, a space module splashes down in the ocean. Parachutes were needed to slow its descent.

▼ Ask an adult to help make a parachute out of tissue paper following this pattern.

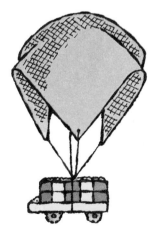

Fix paper hole reinforcers over the holes in the four corners of the parachute. Attach the truck with thread knotted through the corners. If you cut a round hole in the centre of the tissue paper, what happens? Is it easier to hit the target?

11

FABULOUS FLYING MACHINES

Can a sheet of paper fly? Of course it can. But it must be the right shape so that it can cut through the air.

▶ Start with a rectangular sheet of paper and fold it into a dart shape like this.

If you fold flaps at the end of the wings, you can control the path of the dart. Can you make it turn to the right? As the air moves past the flaps, it pushes on the dart, changing its direction.

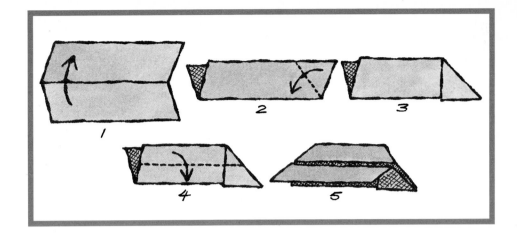

Just like a paper dart, aeroplanes are **streamlined** but they have **engines** to push them. The air moves faster over the wings than under them because of their shape. Air moving quickly has less push than air moving slowly, so the wing is pulled upwards. Birds like gulls flap their wings and fly in a similar way.

◀ Glue some thread to two ping-pong balls and hang them about five centimetres apart from the back of a chair. Ask a friend if she can move the balls together without touching them. Can you think how to do it using moving air?

All you have to do is blow between the balls and they will move together. Try it.

HOT AIR RISING

Warm air is lighter than cold air. Just like a bubble of air floating to the surface in water, warm air rises. Indoors, the warm air cools when it reaches the ceiling and then sinks down again.

You can use rising air to power a spinning snake. Trace this shape on to thin card and cut it out. Fix a pencil on top of a hot radiator with a blob of modelling clay and balance the snake on top.

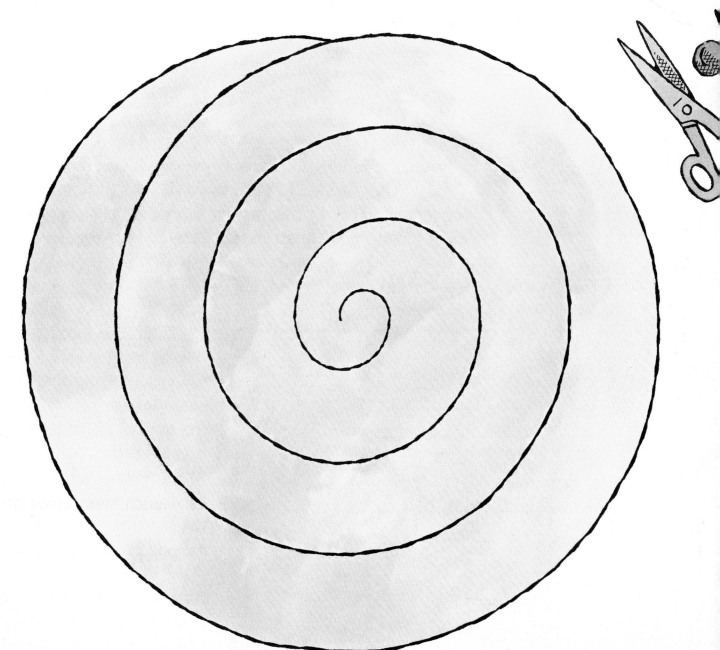

► As the air next to the radiator heats up, it begins to rise and make the snake turn around. Colour your snake to make it more lifelike. You could also give it a forked tongue.

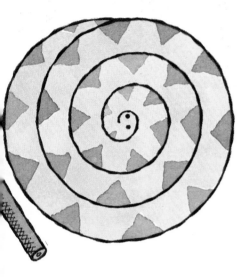

◄ Hang-gliders use rising air to stay up in the sky. They do not have engines, so they must find a column of hot, rising air (called a thermal) to stay up. Do you think gliding would be easier on a hot day or a cold day?

Have you ever watched hang-gliders? They must find a high hill where they can launch themselves into the air and where the warm thermals will keep them gliding for a long time. The pilot hangs from a harness and steers the glider with a control bar.

TRAPPING AIR TO KEEP WARM

Have you ever noticed how a pot of tea will go cold if it is left for some time? Where do you think the heat goes? It is taken away by air currents moving past. Can you think how to stop the air currents?

▲ If someone is cooking in a kitchen you can sometimes see steam rising into the air from very hot water in a saucepan. Do you think the steam could be taking some heat away with it? What do you think would happen if a lid were put on the saucepan? Would it keep the water hot for longer?

◀ In some countries it is very cold, and people have to keep warm and stop heat escaping from their body. They wear special clothes that trap a layer of air next to their skin. This stops the warm air from escaping and taking the heat with it.

▲ Animals must keep warm as well. These polar bears live where there is plenty of ice and snow. They grow very thick fur in several layers to trap air next to their skin.

▶ Ducks spend much of their time in cold water. They have waterproof feathers on the outside to keep out the water and fluffy feathers close to their body to keep in the warm air. Ducks spend a lot of time looking after their feathers to keep them in good condition.

HOT-AIR BALLOONS

About two hundred years ago, the Montgolfier brothers in France noticed that smoke and **steam** move upwards. They thought that if they could trap some hot air in a large balloon, it should be able to fly.

▶ In September 1783 the brothers made a huge balloon out of very light material and carefully started a fire underneath it. No person had ever flown before, so the first passengers of the **hot-air balloon** were a sheep, a chicken and a duck. The first flight was a great success except that the sheep trod on the chicken!

▼ Make your own hot-air balloon. Ask an adult to cut out six shapes like this from tissue paper and then carefully glue them together along the sides but leaving the bottom edges open.

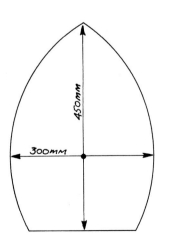

▶ Now ask an adult to fill the balloon with hot air from a hair drier and watch what happens.

WIND POWER

When the Sun shines, it heats up the land and the air above it. The hot air then rises. Cold air rushes in to take the place of the hot air. We call this wind. Wind is a very strong air current but there are smaller movements in the air as well, rather like slow and fast-moving currents in water.

On a windy day you can see the air moving the leaves and branches on trees and feel it tugging at your clothes. The wind has a lot of **energy** and this energy can be used to do useful things.

◄ For centuries, people have used **windmills** to pump water and grind grain. This modern windfarm uses rows of windmills to turn the wind's energy into electricity for the local community.

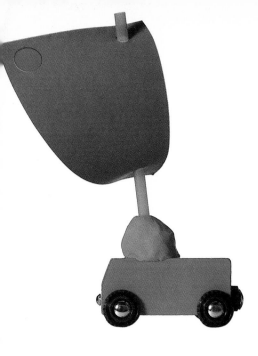

You can have great fun using wind energy to power races with your friends. Make model **land yachts** like these out of old toy cars, some modelling clay, straws and some thin card for the sails. Experiment with sails of different sizes and shapes. Which sails make the land yachts go fastest?

See if the yacht moves faster still when you blow on the sail through a straw. Try moving the yacht by blowing gusts of air from a fan on to the sail. Which way works best?

PUTTING OUT THE LIGHT

Air is really a mixture of different **gases**. One of these gases is **oxygen**. When something burns, it needs oxygen. If there is not enough oxygen, the fire will go out.

▼ Here is a trick that puts out a candle flame, as if by magic. You will need a deep bowl, a short candle, vinegar and bicarbonate of soda.

Fix the candle in the centre of the bowl and sprinkle about one tablespoon of bicarbonate of soda around it. Ask an adult to light the candle.

Never play with fire or matches without telling an adult first.

How can you possibly put out the candle without blowing on the flame? Simple: just pour a small amount of vinegar on to the bicarbonate of soda and watch.

As soon as the vinegar touches the bicarbonate of soda it suddenly foams and gives off a gas that puts out fire. You cannot see the gas but it is heavier than air, so it slowly starts to fill the bowl, instead of floating away. As soon as the gas reaches the candle flame, the light is mysteriously put out.

The gas that you have made is called **carbon dioxide**. These trainee firefighters are learning how to use carbon dioxide foam to put out a fire.

SOUNDS FUN

When an object such as a drum is tapped, its surface quivers and releases very fast shaking movements called **vibrations**. You cannot see them, but the vibrations travel through the air to your ears, where you hear them as **sounds**.

▶ Make a cone from thick paper. Ask a friend to shout from the other side of the garden. Can you hear best with the narrow end to your ear or the wide end?

▲ Tie a spoon to a length of string and hold the ends of the string in your ears. Give a spoon to a friend and ask her to tap your spoon. What can you hear through the string?

▲ Ask an adult to make holes through the bottoms of two yogurt pots. Push a length of string through the holes. Knot the ends so they do not slip through. Ask a friend to hold one pot and walk away from her to pull the string tight. Put your pot to your ear and ask her to speak into the other pot. You now have a portable telephone.

◀ Hold a balloon filled with water next to your ear. Ask your friend to hold a ticking watch against it on the other side. Can you still hear the ticking through the water?

▼ Strike a triangle to make a loud ringing sound. What happens if you touch it?

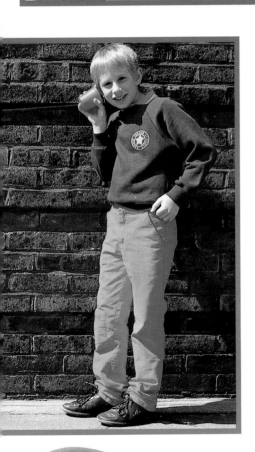

◀ Have you ever noticed that you see lightning before you hear **thunder**? This is because it takes time for the sound to reach you through the air. You can work out how far away the lightning is. When you see the flash, count the seconds until you hear the bang. Divide by 3 and you have the distance in kilometres.

MAKING MUSIC

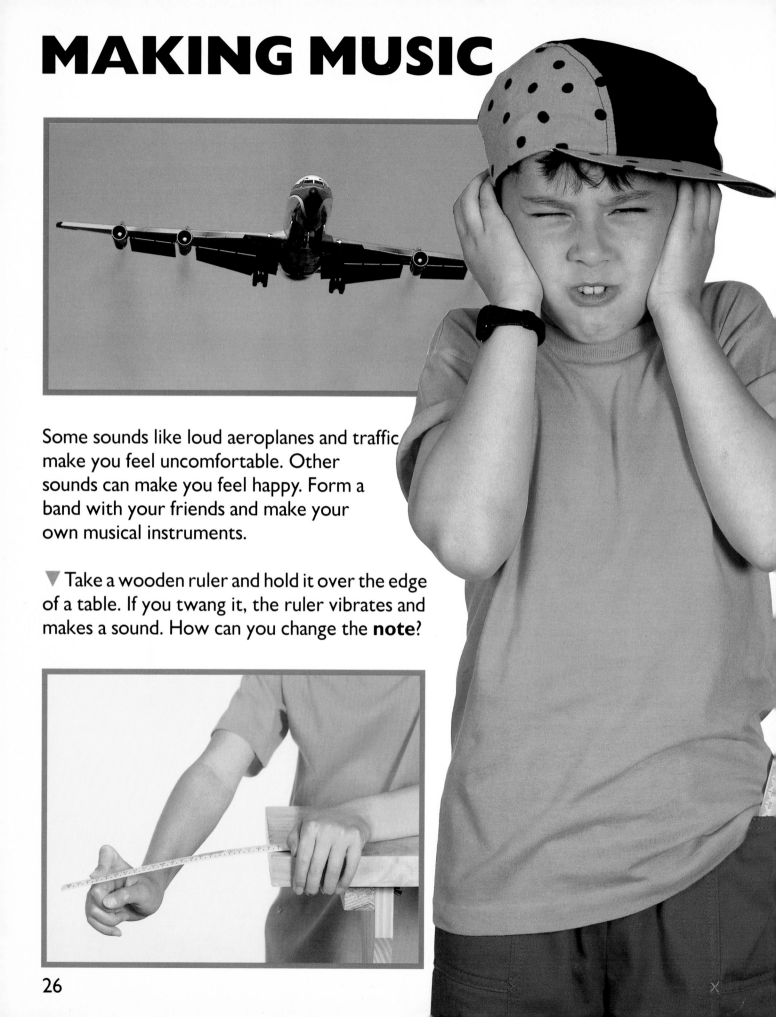

Some sounds like loud aeroplanes and traffic make you feel uncomfortable. Other sounds can make you feel happy. Form a band with your friends and make your own musical instruments.

▼ Take a wooden ruler and hold it over the edge of a table. If you twang it, the ruler vibrates and makes a sound. How can you change the **note**?

◀ Stick some brown paper tightly over a box. When you hit the paper with a wooden stick or ruler, it sounds like a drum. Make some big drums and some little ones. Can you put them in order of high and low sounds?

▼ Use some large saucepan lids, one in each hand, to make a clashing pair of cymbals.

▼ Make an instrument from glass bottles filled with water. If you gently tap the side of a bottle it makes

a nice sound. Try it out for yourself. You can make different notes by changing the depth of water in the bottles.

◀ You can also make an instrument with a row of glasses filled with different levels of water. Wet your index finger and rub it quickly around the top of the glass until you hear a ringing sound. Each glass will give you a different musical note.

PANPIPES AND GUITAR

Here are some more instruments to make.

▶ Fold some tracing paper over a comb, touch the comb gently to your lips and hum a tune.

▼ To make a set of panpipes, ask an adult to cut some old hose-pipe to different lengths and glue or tape them together on a piece of card in order of size. Close one end of each section with some thin card. If you blow across the top of each section it makes a good whistling noise. Which makes the highest note?

▼ To make your own guitar you need a long thin box. Glue a rectangle of card across its width and stretch elastic bands of different thicknesses along its length, so that they rest on the card. Pluck the elastic bands and they vibrate and make a noise. Can you see how to get different notes? The long, thick bands give much lower, deeper notes.

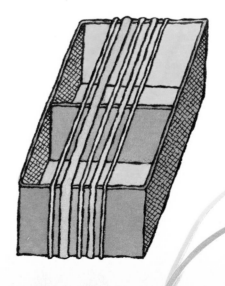

Paint all your musical instruments in different colours. Make music with your friends and play away.

GLOSSARY

Air is the mixture of oxygen and other gases which humans and animals breathe, and which makes up the Earth's atmosphere.

Atmosphere is the gases that surround the Earth.

Breathing is taking air into our lungs so that we can live.

Carbon dioxide is a gas in the air that plants use to make food, and that is used to put out certain fires.

Energy is needed by all things to be active.

Engine is the part of a machine that gives it the power to work.

Firefighters are trained to put out fires as their job.

Gas is a substance like air that is not liquid or solid.

Gravity is a force that pulls things to the ground.

Helicopter is a flying machine with rotating blades that help it to stay up in the air.

Hot-air balloon is a giant balloon filled with hot air that can carry people. Hot air is lighter than cool air and so the balloon lifts easily.

Land yacht is a go-kart with a sail.

Note is a musical sound.

Oxygen is the gas that humans and most animals need to live.

Parachute is a big sail that a person uses when falling from a great height, usually from an aeroplane. It stops him or her from falling to the ground too quickly.

Propeller is a whirling blade that pushes an aeroplane forwards.

Sky-diver is someone who jumps out of high-flying planes, while wearing a parachute.

Sound is any sort of noise.

Steam is small water droplets in the air.

Streamlined means shaped to travel smoothly through liquid or air.

Thunder and lightning are the rumbling sounds and flashes of light that can be seen and heard in some storms.

Vibration is a very fast shaking movement.

Weight is the force with which something pushes downwards.

Wind is moving air.

Windmills are buildings with large sails that turn in the wind. This provides the power to grind corn, pump water or make electricity.

INDEX